MARRIAGE LINES

NOTES OF A STUDENT HUSBAND

OGDEN NASH

MARRIAGE LINES

NOTES OF A STUDENT HUSBAND

Illustrated by
ISADORE SELTZER

LITTLE, BROWN AND COMPANY • BOSTON • TORONTO

The following selections originally appeared in *The New Yorker:*

"They Won't Believe, on New Year's Eve, That New Year's Day
Will Come What May"

"How Can Echo Answer What Echo Cannot Hear?"

"The Middle"

"How to Be Married Without a Spouse, *or* Mr. Kipling, What
Have You Done with Mr. Hauksbee?"

Published simultaneously in Canada
by Little, Brown & Company (Canada) Limited

PRINTED IN THE UNITED STATES OF AMERICA

CONTENTS

FOREWORD

AFTER a third of a century of marriage I find myself still a student husband. I have done my reading,
my research and my homework; I have tangled with
trial and error, theory and practice. Experiment for
experiment, I will match my record with that of
Madame Curie or Dr. Salk. Yet today I feel as far
from my diploma as on that afternoon in June when
I stood at the altar in a state of mingled triumph
and trepidation. As my own examiner I have given
myself passing marks in a tidy number of tests, but
I have had to flunk myself in too many others; there
still remains an alarming host of subjects in which I
have a vast amount of work to make up simply to
stay in the class.

I have the best of reasons for wanting to be gradu-
ated, if not with honors, with at least a respectable
degree. At a dinner dance in November of 1928 I
surreptitiously shifted my place card at the table
while my hostess's back was turned so that I might
sit next to a girl I had met during cocktails. For-

tunately she did not realize that I had substituted myself for her allotted companion, a rich and handsome former Princeton fullback, and I was able to attract her attention with well-phrased laudatory remarks about Al Smith and P. G. Wodehouse, remarks which changed imperceptibly into other and more personal compliments. My aim was then, as it is now, to persuade her to stay beside me for the rest

of my life. In this I have so far succeeded, though there have been moments when she must have rebelled against being the major course selected for self-improvement by a perpetual undergraduate. Still here she is, here we are, and I have hope for the future, since I can now call up the fascination of the grandchildren to reinforce my own fading charms.

It has occurred to me that my notes jotted down through the years might help other student husbands. All of them have been printed before in publications available to the general as well as the scholarly reader, but they are here gathered together for the first time, presented in rough chronological order. Most of them are the result of long and earnest observation of the endearing but baffling feminine charm of one wife in particular and the equally baffling non-masculine peculiarities of many wives in general. I believe that the myopia and obtuseness of the observer increase rather than decrease the value of his notes. In the matter of wives, to know all is to be forgiven nothing. An occasionally lucky guess as to what makes a wife tick is the best a man can hope for, and even then, no sooner has he learned how to cope with the tick than she tocks. She is also likely to strike 11 at 6 o'clock and turn out to be right because she was thinking in terms of Paris time.

There are no conclusions here, only winding approaches to conclusions, but the endless search for knowledge has been an exceptionally happy one. The same, dear fellow students, to you.

MARRIAGE LINES

NOTES OF A STUDENT HUSBAND

LOVE UNDER THE
REPUBLICANS
(OR DEMOCRATS)

Come live with me and be my love
And we will all the pleasures prove
Of a marriage conducted with economy
In the Twentieth Century Anno Donomy.
We'll live in a dear little walk-up flat
With practically room to swing a cat
And a potted cactus to give it hauteur
And a bathtub equipped with dark brown water.
We'll eat, without undue discouragement,
Foods low in cost but high in nouragement
And quaff with pleasure, while chatting wittily,
The peculiar wine of Little Italy.
We'll remind each other it's smart to be thrifty
And buy our clothes for something-fifty.
We'll bus for miles on holidays
For seats at depressing matinees,
And every Sunday we'll have a lark
And take a walk in Central Park.
And one of these days not too remote
You'll probably up and cut my throat.

A WORD TO BUSYBODIES

You cannot cure the lovelorn lover's insomnia
By shouting at him, AMOR VINCIT OMNIA.

THAT REMINDS ME

Just imagine yourself seated on a shadowy terrace,
And beside you is a girl who stirs you more strangely
    than an heiress.
It is a summer evening at its most superb,
And the moonlight reminds you that To Love is an
    active verb,
And your hand clasps hers, which rests there without
    shrinking,
And after a silence fraught with romance you ask her
    what she is thinking,
And she starts and returns from the moon-washed
    distances to the shadowy veranda,
And says, Oh I was wondering how many bamboo
    shoots a day it takes to feed a baby Giant Panda.
Or you stand with her on a hilltop and gaze on a
    winter sunset,
And everything is as starkly beautiful as a page from
    Sigrid Undset,
And your arm goes around her waist and you make
    an avowal which for masterfully marshaled
    emotional content might have been a page of
    Ouida's or Thackeray's,
And after a silence fraught with romance she says, I
    forgot to order the limes for the Daiquiris.
Or in a twilight drawing room you have just asked
    the most momentous of questions,

And after a silence fraught with romance she says, I
think this little table would look better where
that little table is, but then where would that
little table go, have you any suggestions?
And that's the way they go around hitting below our
belts ;
It isn't that nothing is sacred to them, it's just that
at the Sacred Moment they are always thinking
of something else.

SONG FOR PIER SOMETHING
OR OTHER

Steamer, steamer, outward bound,
Couldn't you, wouldn't you turn around?
Mightn't you double on your track?
Mightn't you possibly bring her back?
No, says the steamer, no, no, no!
We go, says the steamer, go, go, go!
Who, says the steamer, who are you?
Boo! says the steamer.
Boo!

Steamer, steamer, are you sure
You can carry her secure?
Emerge from ice and storm and fog
With an uneventful log?
Chance, says the steamer, I am chance!
Chance, says the steamer, that's romance!
Who, says the steamer, who are you?
Boo! says the steamer.
Boo!

Steamer, steamer, hard and splendid,
Goddess unwittingly offended,
Are the males who prowl your decks
Attractive to the other sex?
Wait, says the steamer, sit and wait.

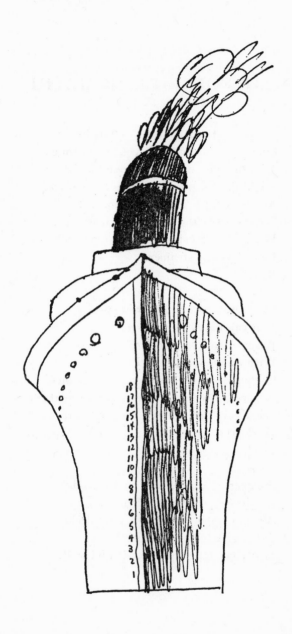

Fate, says the steamer, I am Fate.
Who, says the steamer, who are you?
Boo! says the steamer.
Boo!

Steamer, cogitate awhile
Before you smile your final smile.
Seven days are yours to mock;
Steamer, wait until you dock.
Wait till she is safe ashore,
Steamer I do not adore!
Boo, says the steamer, and double boo!
Who, says the steamer,
Are you?

Steamer, steamer, I am he
Whose *raison d'être* you bore to sea.
Steamer, lightly you weighed your anchor.
Try so lightly to weigh my rancor.
As soon as she is safely off you
I'll curse you from Sandy Hook to Corfu.

You who carried her off so boldly
Shall pay for it hotly, pay for it coldly,
With fog and howling hurricanes,
And icebergs in the shipping lanes,
And strikes of longshoremen and tugs,
And a passenger list of jitter bugs —
Pooh! says the steamer. Pooh for you!
Toodle-de-oodle-de-oo!

9

ABSENCE MAKES THE HEART
GROW HEART TROUBLE

I know a girl who is in Paris, France,
And I fear that every evening she goes out to dance,
And she ought to be pining for the undersigned,
But I fear that nothing is further from her mind,
And what is very suspicious, her letters say that she
    is being very quiet,
But my nerves deny it,
And I am unhappily sure that she is drinking cham-
    pagne with aristocrats,
And exchanging cynicisms with sophistocrats.
She goes walking in the Bois
With elegant young men who are not *moi*.
She is receiving compliments from ambassadors,
And riding in *fiacres* with foreign agents who cry
    that for her they would betray the secrets of
    their lords and massadors.
Artists to have her pose for them are clamoring,
Tenors and symphony conductors tempt her with
    their entire repertoire from *Pagliacci to Göt-
    terdämmerung;*
Argentines and Brazilians
Seek to dazzle her with their dazzling millions;

Men of the world with etchings and monocles
Plead with her to become part of their personal
   chronicles;
Aides and equerries try to explain without too much
   bluntness and yet without too much shyness
The advantages a girl or a tailor enjoys when he or
   she is entitled to the subtitle of By Appointment
   to His Royal Highness.
Trips abroad are very nice for Davis Cup teams and
   Olympic teams, and that's about all you can say
   for them,
Because I think that when you are fond of somebody
   you would rather be with them than away from
   them,
So I wish that time would suddenly advance,
Because I want to be standing on the dock trying to
   find somebody on deck who will undoubtedly be
   wearing a terribly smart and perfectly terrible
   hat which she bought in Paris, France.

ALWAYS MARRY
AN APRIL GIRL

Praise the spells and bless the charms,
I found April in my arms.
April golden, April cloudy,
Gracious, cruel, tender, rowdy;
April soft in flowered languor,
April cold with sudden anger,
Ever changing, ever true —
I love April, I love you.

ASIDE TO HUSBANDS

What do you do when you've wedded a girl all legal
   and lawful,
And she goes around saying she looks awful?
When she makes deprecatory remarks about her
   format,

And claims that her hair looks like a doormat?

When she swears that the complexion of which you
are so fond

Looks like the bottom of a dried-up pond?

When she for whom your affection is not the least
like Plato's

Compares her waist to a badly tied sack of potatoes?

Oh, who wouldn't rather be on a flimsy bridge with a
hungry lion at one end and a hungry tiger at
the other end and hungry crocodiles underneath

Than confronted by their dearest making remarks
about her own appearance through clenched
teeth?

Why won't they believe that the reason they find
themselves the mother of your children is because you think of all the looks in the world,
their looks are the nicest?

Why must we continue to be thus constantly ordealed
and crisised?

I think it high time these hoity-toity ladies were made
to realize that when they impugn their face and
their ankles and their waist

They are thereby insultingly impugning their taste-
ful husbands' impeccable taste.

A LADY THINKS SHE
IS THIRTY

Unwillingly Miranda wakes,
Feels the sun with terror,
One unwilling step she takes,
Shuddering to the mirror.

Miranda in Miranda's sight
Is old and gray and dirty;
Twenty-nine she was last night;
This morning she is thirty.

Shining like the morning star,
Like the twilight shining,
Haunted by a calendar,
Miranda sits a-pining.

Silly girl, silver girl,
Draw the mirror toward you;
Time who makes the years to whirl
Adorned as he adored you.

Time is timelessness for you;
Calendars for the human;

What's a year, or thirty, to
Loveliness made woman?

Oh, Night will not see thirty again,
Yet soft her wing, Miranda;
Pick up your glass and tell me, then —
How old is Spring, Miranda?

I DO, I WILL, I HAVE

How wise I am to have instructed the butler to instruct the first footman to instruct the second
footman to instruct the doorman to order my
carriage;

I am about to volunteer a definition of marriage.

Just as I know that there are two Hagens, Walter
and Copen,

I know that marriage is a legal and religious alliance
entered into by a man who can't sleep with the
window shut and a woman who can't sleep with
the window open.

Moreover, just as I am unsure of the difference between flora and fauna and flotsam and jetsam,

I am quite sure that marriage is the alliance of two
people one of whom never remembers birthdays
and the other never forgetsam,

And he refuses to believe there is a leak in the water
pipe or the gas pipe and she is convinced she is
about to asphyxiate or drown,

And she says, Quick get up and get my hairbrushes
off the window sill, it's raining in, and he replies,
Oh they're all right, its only raining straight
down.

That is why marriage is so much more interesting
  than divorce,
Because it's the only known example of the happy
  meeting of the immovable object and the irre-
  sistible force.
So I hope husbands and wives will continue to debate
  and combat over everything debatable and com-
  batable,
Because I believe a little incompatibility is the spice
  of life, particularly if he has income and she is
  pattable.

CONFESSION TO BE TRACED
ON A BIRTHDAY CAKE

Lots of people are richer than me,
Yet pay a slenderer tax;
Their annual levy seems to wane
While their income seems to wax.
Lots of people have stocks and bonds
To further their romances;
I've cashed my ultimate Savings Stamp —
But nobody else has Frances.

Lots of people are stronger than me,
And greater athletic menaces;
They poise like gods on diving boards
And win their golfs and tennises.
Lots of people have lots more grace
And cut fine figures at dances,
While I was born with galoshes on —
But nobody else has Frances.

Lots of people are wiser than me,
And carry within their cranium
The implications of Stein and Joyce
And the properties of uranium.
They know the mileage to every star

In the heaven's vast expanses;
I'm inclined to believe that the world is flat —
But nobody else has Frances.

Speaking of wisdom and wealth and grace —
As recently I have dared to —
There are lots of people compared to whom
I'd rather not be compared to.
There are people I ought to wish I was;
But under the circumstances,
I prefer to continue my life as me —
For nobody else has Frances.

WHAT ALMOST EVERY
WOMAN KNOWS
SOONER OR LATER

Husbands are things that wives have to get used to
 putting up with,
And with whom they breakfast with and sup with.
They interfere with the discipline of nurseries,
And forget anniversaries,
And when they have been particularly remiss
They think they can cure everything with a great big
 kiss,
And when you tell them about something they have
 done they just look unbearably patient and
 smile a superior smile,
And think, Oh she'll get over it after a while.
And they always drink cocktails faster than they can
 assimilate them,
And if you look in their direction they act as if they
 were martyrs and you were trying to sacrifice,
 or immolate them.
And they never want to get up or go to bed at the
 same time as you do,
And when you perform some simple rite like putting
 cold cream on your face or applying a touch of
 lipstick they seem to think you are up to some
 kind of black magic like a priestess of Voodoo,

And they are brave and calm and cool and collected
about the ailments of the person they have
promised to honor and cherish,
But the minute they get a sniffle or a stomachache of
their own, why you'd think they were about to
perish,
And when you are alone with them they ignore all the
minor courtesies, and as for airs and graces
they utterly lack them,
But when there are a lot of people around they hand
you so many chairs and ashtrays and sand-
wiches and butter you with such bowings and
scrapings that you want to smack them.
Husbands are indeed an irritating form of life,
And yet through some quirk of Providence most of
them are really very deeply ensconced in the
affection of their wife.

TIN WEDDING WHISTLE

Though you know it anyhow
Listen to me, darling, now,

Proving what I need not prove,
How I know I love you, love.

Near and far, near and far,
I am happy where you are;

Likewise I have never larnt
How to be it where you aren't.

Far and wide, far and wide,
I can walk with you beside;

Furthermore, I tell you what,
I sit and sulk where you are not.

Visitors remark my frown
When you're upstairs and I am down,

In fact I care not where you be,
Just as long as it's with me.

In all your absences I glimpse
Fire and flood and trolls and imps.

Is your train a minute slothful?
I goad the stationmaster wrothful.

When with friends to bridge you drive
I never know if you're alive,

And when you linger late in shops
I long to telephone the cops.

Yet how worth the waiting for,
To see you coming through the door.

Somehow, I can be complacent
Never but with you adjacent.

Near and far, near and far,
I am happy where you are;

Likewise, I have never larnt
How to be it where you aren't.

Then grudge me not my fond endeavor,
To hold you in my sight forever;

Yes, and I'm afraid I pout
When I'm indoors and you are out;

But how contentedly I view
Any room containing you.

Let none, not even you, disparage
Such valid reason for a marriage.

JUST WRAP IT UP, AND
I'LL THROW IT AWAY LATER

Men think that men have more sense than women and
　　women think that any woman has more sense
　　than any man,
An issue which I eagerly evade, for who am I to pass
　　judgment on the comparative reasoning proc-
　　esses of, say, Mr. Lunt and Miss Fontanne?
However, I ask you to visualize, please, a clear-think-
　　ing American male who needs a hat, or a left
　　sock, or an ashtray in the form of the statue
　　Civic Virtue by the sculptor MacMonnies,
And what does he do, he goes into the likeliest shop
　　and buys it and returns to the regular evening
　　race with the children for first go at the funnies.
Kindly contrast this with the procedure of his wife
　　or sister or aunt who drops into a store for
　　three ounces of flax for the spinning wheel or an
　　extra minuet for the spinet,
And what happens, the doorstep is crawling for days
　　with people delivering lampshades and bed-
　　spreads and dirndls and chairs that expand into
　　bridge tables and bridge tables that expand into
　　chaises longues, and husbands who can't bear it
　　simply have to grin it.

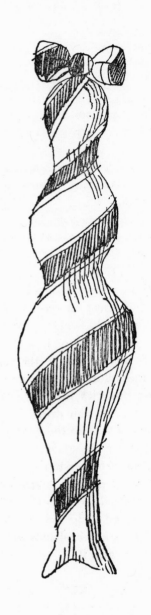

Man's idea of shopping is to buy what he needs and
get through with it.

Woman's idea is to have everything she has never
needed sent home and then figure out what to do
with it.

It is as true today as in the day of David and Goliath
or Corbett and Fitzsimmons,

That men go into a shop to supply a want, and
women principally to stimulate their imaginations, but men's imaginations need no extra
stimulus as long as their world is filled with
beautiful unanswerable womens.

IF ANYTHING SHOULD ARISE,
IT ISN'T I

A prepared position Man hankers for
Is parallel to and above the floor,
For thither retreating horizontally,
He evades the issues that charge him frontally.
But pumpkins do not burgeon in Maytime,
And bed is out of bounds in daytime.
A man in pajamas after nine
Transgresses the housewife's Party Line.
He's unethical and unpatriotic,
Unkempt, uncouth, unaristocrotic,
Unwept, unhonored, unsung, unread,
And, if he doesn't get up, unfed.
That is why he smiles when the moment comes
When hands are hot and forehead hums,
When throat is parched and nostrils rankle
And legs are aching from knee to ankle.
Making sure the housewife observes his plight,
He bravely whispers he's quite all right,
What's a spot of fever, a spell of dizziness.
Where's his hat, he is off to business.
So she telephones the office for him,
And stoups of lemonade doth pour him,

And trees his shoes and hangs his clothes up
And introduces drops his nose up,
She fetches toast as light as froth,
And bouillon, consommé and broth,
And be he Harvardite or Yaleite,
She orders him to bed by daylight,
Like Heaven chastening a Baalite
She orders him to bed by daylight.
Beneath the sheets he cracks his knuckles
And chokes to cover up his chuckles,
And coughs a spirited cadenza
In grateful praise of influenza.

DON'T EVEN TELL YOUR
WIFE, PARTICULARLY

All good men believe that women would rather get rid
of a piece of gossip than a bulge,
And all good women believe that gossip is a feminine
weakness in which men never indulge.
Rather than give ear to scandalous rumors,
Why, men would rather play golf in bloomers,
And rather than talk behind each other's backs,
They would go shopping in a mink coat and slacks.
It is one of each sex's uniquenesses
That men's talk is all of humanity's aspirations, and
women's all of their friends' weaknesses.
Yes, this is a universal credo that no amount of evi-
dence can alter,
Including that of Petronius, Suetonius, Pepys, Bos-
well, the locker room of the country club, and
Mrs. Winchell's little boy, Walter.
Allow me to ask and answer one question before de-
parting for Mount Everest or Lake Ossipee:
Who says men aren't gossipy? — Men say men aren't
gossipy.

APARTMENT TO SUBLET — UNFURNISHED

The Murrays are hunting a house,
They are tired of living in flats.
They long for a personal mouse
And a couple of personal cats.
They are hunting a house to inhabit,
An Eden, or even an Arden,
They are thinking of keeping a rabbit,
They are thinking of digging a garden.
How giddy the Murrays have grown
To aspire to a house of their own!

Oh, hurry, hurry!
Says Mrs. Murray.
Tarry awhile, says he,
If you care for a house
As is a house,
You'd better leave it to me.
I'd like an orchard, apple or peach,
I'd like an accessible bathing beach,
And a den for unwinding detective plots,
And a lawn for practicing mashie shots,
And open fires,
And a pleasant sunroom,

A handy garage,
And perhaps a gunroom,
And an atmosphere exempt of static,
And a furnace silent and automatic.
For such a house
I would hurry, hurry —
I'm a practical man,
Says Mr. Murray.

The Murrays of 17 B,
The Murrays are going away
From the wireless in 17 C,
And the parties in 17 A.
For the Murrays are tired of flats,
They are rapidly growing aloof
As they dream of their personal cats,
As they dream of their personal roof.
Their friends cannot smother their merriment
When they speak of the Murrays' experiment.

Oh, hurry, hurry!
Says Mr. Murray.
Tarry awhile, says she.
When we choose a house,
Let us choose a house
As nice as a house can be.
With a dozen windows south and east,
And a dozen capacious cupboards at least,
And a laundry lilting with light and air,
And a porch for a lady to dry her hair,

And plenty of sun,
And plenty of shade,
And a neat little place
For a possible maid,
And a wall with roses clambering wild,
And a quiet room for a sleepy child.
If you happen to see it,
Hurry, hurry!
For *that's* the house,
Says Mrs. Murray.

YOU HAVE MORE FREEDOM
IN A HOUSE

The Murrays are snug in their house,
They are finished forever with flats;
They longed for a personal mouse
And room to swing dozens of cats.
They longed for a hearth and a doorway,
In Arden, or maybe in Eden,
But the Eden is rather like Norway,
And the Arden like winter in Sweden.
How baffled the Murrays have grown
Since they live in a house of their own!

Oh, hurry, hurry!
Says Mrs. Murray.
But listen, my dear, says he,
If you want the house
A temperate house,
You'd better not leave it to me.
I've learned the knack of swinging a cat,
But I can't coerce the thermostat.
The furnace has given a gruesome cough,
And something has cut the fuel off,
And the heart of the nursery radiator
Is cold as the prose of Walter Pater,
And I've telephoned for the service men

But they can't get here until after ten,
So swaddle the children
And hurry, hurry —
I'm a practical man,
Says Mr. Murray.

The Murrays are vague about fuses
And mechanical matters like that,
And each of them frequently muses
On the days when they lived in a flat.
Was the plumbing reluctant to plumb?
Was the climate suggestive of Canada?
Did the radio crackle and hum?
You simply called down to the janitor!
The Murrays have found no replacement
For the genius who lived in the basement.

Oh, hurry, hurry!
Says Mr. Murray.
I'm doing my best, says she,
But it's hard to scrub
In a tepid tub,
So the guests must wait for me;
And tell them they'll get their cocktails later
When you've managed to fix the refrigerator.
And explain if the coffee looks like water
That the stove is as queer as a seventh daughter,
And I will be down as soon as able
To unstick the drawers of my dressing table.

There's a car at the door, says Mrs. Murray,
The doorbell's broken, so hurry, hurry!
Oh, I don't regret
Being wed to you,
But I wish I could wed
A janitor too.

I'M SURE SHE SAID
SIX-THIRTY

One of the hardest explanations to be found
Is an explanation for just standing around.
Anyone just standing around looks pretty sinister,
Even a minister;
Consider then the plight of the criminal,
Who lacks even the protective coloration of a hym-
    inal,
And as just standing around is any good criminal's
    practically daily stint,
I wish to proffer a hint.
Are you, sir, a masher who blushes as he loiters,
Do you stammer to passersby that you are merely
    expecting a streetcar, or a dispatch from Reu-
    ter's?
Or perhaps you are a safeblower engaged in casing a
    joint;
Can you look the patrolman in the eye or do you
    forget all the savoir-faire you ever loint?
Suppose you are a shoplifter awaiting an opportun-
    ity to lift a shop,
Or simply a novice with a length of lead pipe killing
    time in a dark alley pending the arrival of a
    wealthy fop,

41

Well, should any official ask you why you are just
     standing around,
Do you wish you could simply sink into the ground?
My dear sir, do not be embarrassed, do not reach for
     your gun or your knife,
Remember the password, which, uttered in a tone of
     quiet despair, is the explanation of anyone's
     standing around anywhere at any hour for any
     length of time: "I'm waiting for my wife."

TO A LADY PASSING TIME
BETTER LEFT UNPASSED

O lady of the lucent hair,
Why do you play at solitaire?
What imp, what demon misanthrope,
Prompted this session of lonely hope?
What boredom drives you, and great Lord!
How can such as you be bored?
The gleaming world awaits your eye
While you essay futility.
That mouth is shaped for livelier sport
Than paging of a pasteboard court —
Why, even the Red Knave longing lingers,
While Black Queens wait, in those white fingers.
See now the joy that lights your face
Squandered on some fortuitous ace,
Where formerly dark anger burned
When a five perverse would not be turned.
O, know you not, that darkling frown
Could topple Caesar's empire down;
That quick, bright joy, if flashed on men,
Could sudden build it up again?
Get up! Get up! Throw down the pack!
Rise in your gown of shining black!

Withdraw, my dear, while you are able
The slender feet from 'neath the table;
Remove from the regretful baize
The elbows curved in cunning ways.
Is there no game that pleasure brings
But fretting over painted things?
No gay, ecstatic end in view
But shuffle and begin anew?
Get up, I tell you, girl, get up!
Wine keeps not ever in the cup;
Music is mortal, comes a day
When the musicians will not play;
Even love immortal, love undying,
Finds the loved one's Patience trying.
Let two-and-fifty rivals hiss me —
For God's sake, girl, come here and kiss me!

I NEVER EVEN SUGGESTED IT

I know lots of men who are in love and lots of men
    who are married and lots of men who are both,
And to fall out with their loved ones is what all of
    them are most loth.
They are conciliatory at every opportunity,
Because all they want is serenity and a certain
    amount of impunity.
Yes, many the swain who has finally admitted that
    the earth is flat
Simply to sidestep a spat,
Many the masculine Positively or Absolutely which
    has been diluted to an If
Simply to avert a tiff,
Many the two-fisted executive whose domestic con-
    versation is limited to a tactfully interpolated
    Yes,
And then he is amazed to find that he is being raked
    backwards over a bed of coals nevertheless.
These misguided fellows are under the impression
    that it takes two to make a quarrel, that you
    can sidestep a crisis by nonaggression and non-
    resistance,
Instead of removing yourself to a discreet distance.

47

Passivity can be a provoking modus operandi;
Consider the Empire and Gandhi.
Silence is golden, but sometimes invisibility is golder,
Because loved ones may not be able to make bricks
without straw, but often they don't need any
straw to manufacture a bone to pick or a chip
for their soft white shoulder.
It is my duty, gentlemen, to inform you that women
are dictators all, and I recommend to you this
moral:
In real life it takes only one to make a quarrel.

DON'T BE CROSS, AMANDA

Don't be cross, Amanda,
Amanda, don't be cross,
For when you're cross, Amanda,
I feel an albatross
Around my neck, or dank gray moss,
And my eyes assume an impervious gloss.
Amanda,
Dear Amanda,
Don't be cross.

Do not frown, Amanda,
Amanda, do not frown,
For when you frown, Amanda,
I wamble like a clown,
My mouth is stuffed with eiderdown,
And I spatter coffee upon your gown.
Amanda,
Dear Amanda,
Do not frown.

Don't clam up, Amanda,
Amanda, do not clam,
For when you clam, Amanda,
I don't know where I am.
What is it that I did you damn?

Shall I make amends for a sheep, or a lamb?
Amanda,
Dear Amanda,
Do not clam.

Please be gay, Amanda,
Amanda, please be gay,
For when you're gay, Amanda,
The stars come out by day,
The police throw parking tags away,
And I want to kick up my heels and bray.
Amanda,
Dear Amanda,
Please be gay.

THE NYMPH AND THE
SHEPHERD
OR
SHE WENT THAT-A-WAY

Few things are less endearing than a personal com-
  parison,
But I know a lady who is very like the elusive mother
  of Mr. Milne's James James Morrison Morrison.
She would be a perfect wife could she but be re-
  strained by a leash or a fetter,
Because she has the roving tendencies of an Irish
  setter.
Her husband assists her from the cab and stops to
  pay the fare,
And when he turns around she isn't there,
She is a hundred yards off, blithe as a flock of linnets,
And in a fair way to do the mile under four minutes.
He assists her from the train and by the time he has
  caught a porter she is at the top of the moving
  stairway,
And again to do the mile under four minutes she is
  in a fair way.
She shoots ahead of him in London crowds and leaves
  him behind fumbling with lire in Pisa,

Despite the fact that he is in sole possession of all the travelers' checks and their joint passport and visa.

If in the Louvre she exclaims, "Oh, look at the Mona Lisa!" and he pauses to look at the Mona Lisa,

By the time he has looked she is three corners and forty masterpieces away, and himself alone with the same old money and passport and visa.

Sometimes he is touched and flattered by her faith in him, but mostly he feels like Queen Victoria's chair,

Which Queen Victoria never looked behind at before she sat down, because she just knew it would be there.

THE STRANGE CASE OF
MR. ORMANTUDE'S BRIDE

Once there was a bridegroom named Mr. Ormantude
    whose intentions were hard to disparage,
Because he intended to make his a happy marriage,
And he succeeded for going on fifty years,
During which he was in marital bliss up to his ears.
His wife's days and nights were enjoyable
Because he catered to every foible;
He went around humming hymns
And anticipating her whims.
Many a fine bit of repartee died on his lips
Lest it throw her anecdotes into eclipse;
He was always silent when his cause was meritorious,
And he never engaged in argument unless sure he was
    so obviously wrong that she couldn't help emerg-
    ing victorious,
And always when in her vicinity
He was careful to make allowances for her feminin-
    ity;
Were she snappish, he was sweetish,
And of understanding her he made a fetish.
Everybody said his chances of celebrating his golden
    wedding looked good,
But on his golden wedding eve he was competently
    poisoned by his wife who could no longer stand
    being perpetually understood.

A WARNING TO WIVES

"The outcome of the trial is another warning that if you must kill someone, you should spare the person possessing life insurance. . . . Figures are available to show that convictions are much more common in 'insurance murders' than in other types of homicides." — BOSTON HERALD

Speak gently to your husband, ma'am,
And encourage all his sneezes;
That nasty cough may carry him off
If exposed to drafts and breezes.
But suppose the scoundrel lingers on
And insists on being cured;
Well, it isn't a sin if a girl steps in —
Unless the brute's insured.

Oh the selfishness of men, welladay, welladay!
Oh the sissies, oh the softies, oh the mice!
Egotistically they strive to keep themselves alive,
And insurance is their scurviest device.
Insurance!
It's insurance
That tries a lady's temper past endurance.
Yet it's safer, on the whole,

To practice self-control
If there's apt to be a question of insurance.
Arsenic soup is a dainty soup,
But not if he's paid his premium.
Or a .32 in a pinch will do,
If you're bored with the epithalemium.
But to make acquittal doubly sure —
No maybes, no perhapses —

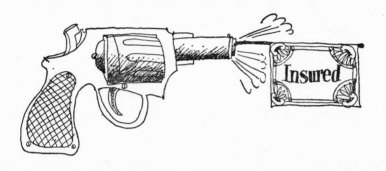

You'll do well to wait to expunge your mate
Until his policy lapses.

The hypocrisy of men, welladay, welladay!
Whited sepulchers are much to be preferred.
They claim it's for their wives they evaluate their
    lives,

But it's fatal if you take them at their word.
Insurance!
Oh insurance!
What holds potential widows fast in durance?
Not the Adlers and the Freuds,
But the Mutuals and Lloyds,
And the jury's evil mind about insurance.

THE PERFECT HUSBAND

He tells you when you've got on too much lipstick,
And helps you with your girdle when your hips stick.

A WORD ABOUT WINTER

Now the frost is on the pane,
Rugs upon the floor again,
Now the screens are in the cellar,
Now the student cons the speller,
Lengthy summer noon is gone,
Twilight treads the heels of dawn,
Round-eyed sun is now a squinter,
Tiptoe breeze a panting sprinter,
Every cloud a blizzard hinter,
Squirrel on the snow a printer,
Rainspout sprouteth icy splinter,
Willy-nilly, this is winter.

Summer-swollen doorjambs settle,
Ponds and puddles turn to metal,
Skater whoops in frisky fettle,
Golf club stingeth like a nettle,
Radiator sings like kettle,
Hearth is Popocatepetl.

Runneth nose and chappeth lip,
Draft evadeth weather strip,
Doctor wrestleth with grippe

In never-ending rivalship.
Rosebush droops in garden shoddy,
Blood is cold and thin in body,
Weary postman dreams of toddy,
Head before the hearth grows noddy.

On the hearth the embers gleam,
Glowing like a maiden's dream,
Now the apple and the oak
Paint the sky with chimney smoke,
Husband now, without disgrace,
Dumps ashtrays in the fireplace.

SUMMER SERENADE

When the thunder stalks the sky,
When tickle-footed walks the fly,
When shirt is wet and throat is dry,
Look, my darling, that's July.

Though the grassy lawn be leather,
And prickly temper tug the tether,
Shall we postpone our love for weather?
If we must melt, let's melt together!

THE STRANGE CASE OF
MR. PALLISER'S PALATE

Once there was a man named Mr. Palliser and he
    asked his wife, May I be a gourmet?
And she said, You sure may,
But she also said, If my kitchen is going to produce
    a Cordon Blue,
It won't be me, it will be you,
And he said, You mean *Cordon Bleu?*
And she said to never mind the pronunciation so long
    as it was him and not *heu.*
But he wasn't discouraged; he bought a white hat
    and *The Cordon Bleu Cook Book* and said, How
    about some *Huîtres en Robe de Chambre?*
And she sniffed and said, Are you reading a cook
    book or *Forever Ambre?*
And he said, Well, if you prefer something more
    Anglo-Saxon,
Why suppose I whip up some tasty *Filets de Sole
    Jackson,*
And she pretended not to hear, so he raised his voice
    and said, Could I please you with some *Pau-
    piettes de Veau à la Grecque* or *Cornets de Jam-
    bon Lucullus* or perhaps some nice *Moules à la
    Bordelaise?*

And she said, Kindly lower your voice or the neigh-
bors will think we are drunk and disordelaise,

And she said, Furthermore the whole idea of your
cooking anything fit to eat is a farce. So what
did Mr. Palliser do then?

Well, he offered her *Oeufs Farcis Maison* and *Hom-
ard Farci St. Jacques* and *Tomate Farcie à la
Bayonne* and *Aubergines Farcies Provençales*,
as well as *Aubergines Farcies Italiennes*,

And she said, Edward, kindly accompany me as usual
to Hamburger Heaven and stop playing the
fool,

And he looked in the book for one last suggestion and
it suggested *Croques Madame*, so he did, and
now he dines every evening on *Crème de Con-
combres Glacée*, *Côtelettes de Volaille Vicom-
tesse*, and *Artichauds à la Barigoule*.

THE VOICE OF EXPERIENCE

A husband at a lecture
Twitches his architecture.

He undergoes the lecturing
Like unanesthetized vivisecturing.

He's a glassy-eyed conjecturer
Of the ancestry of the lecturer.

Husbands hide in storerooms
To escape Town Halls and Forums.

They improvise In Memoriams
For speakers in auditoriums.

They regard as nauseous nostrums
Opinions delivered from rostrums.

They feel about orators' rhetorics
Like Caesar about Vercingetorix.

They flinch as the fog of boredom
Creeps verbosely toredom.

There is none so irate and awkward
As a husband being Chautauquard.

Their collars grow more and more cumbersome
And at last they essay to slumber some.

But this respite their spouses grudge them,
And if they nod, they nudge them.

THE SOLITUDE OF
MR. POWERS

Once there was a lonely man named Mr. Powers.

He was lonely because his wife fixed flowers.

Mr. Powers was a gallant husband, but whenever he
wished to demonstrate his gall*an*try

His beloved was always out with six vases and a
bunch of something or other in the pantry.

He got no conversation while they ate

Because she was always nipping dead blossoms off the
centerpiece and piling them on her plate.

He could get no conversation after meals because if
he happened to begin one

She would look at the mantel and wonder if she
shouldn't switch the small fat vase with the tall
thin one.

Yes, even when she wasn't actually fixing flowers
there was no forgetting about them,

Because before fixing them she was busy cutting
them, and after fixing them she was busy fretting about them.

Mr. Powers began to shave only once a week because
no one cared whether his chin was scratchy;

He felt as lonely as *Cavalleria* without *Pagliacci*.

Finally he said Hey!

I might as well be alone with myself as alone with a
lot of vases that have to have their water re-
plenished every day.

And he walked off into the dawn,

And his wife just kept on refilling vases and never
noticed that he was gone.
Beware of floral arrangements;
They lead to marital estrangements.

HOW TO HARRY A HUSBAND
OR
IS THAT ACCESSORY
REALLY NESSARY?

Husband stands at door of flat,
Coat in elbow, hand on hat,
In his pocket, from broker shady,
Two good seats for *My Fair Lady.*
Patiently he stands there humming,
Coming, darling? Darling, coming?

But she's a freak and she's a hag,
She's got the wrong, she murmurs, bag,
She's got, she adds in wild distress,
To change the bag or change the dress.
She'd as soon appear with stockings ragged
As be seen incongruously bebaggèd.

Husband rings the bell for lift,
Hears it chunk and upward drift,
Well knows taxis in the rain
Rarer than the whooping crane.
Impatiently he stands there snarling,
Darling, coming? Coming, darling?

Another bag at last she chooses
And everything in the first bag loses.
She fumbles with many a dainty curse
For lipstick, glasses, keys, and purse.*
He grunts, as dies preprandial liquor,
To change from the skin out would have been quicker.

They disrupt the middle of the show,
Their seats are middle of the row,
They crawl and climb like tandem tractors
Between the audience and the actors,
Whose delicious rapport might have lagged
Had she been incongruously bebagged.

* Then —
She turns it inside out and scratches
For handkerchief, cigarettes, and matches,
Tweezers, compact, and aspirin,
And Band-Aids redolent of My Sin,
Driver's license and Charga-Plate,
A sweepstake ticket one year late,
A colored chart of a five-day diet,
A Penguin commended by Gilbert Highet,
A tearful appeal from a charitymonger,
And a catalogue from Lewis & Conger.
This is she whose eyes start from their sockets
At the contents of her small son's pockets.

THEY WON'T BELIEVE, ON NEW YEAR'S EVE, THAT NEW YEAR'S DAY WILL COME WHAT MAY

How do I feel today? I feel as unfit as an unfiddle,
And it is the result of a certain turbulence in the
   mind and an uncertain burbulence in the middle.
What was it anyway, that angry thing that flew at
   me?
I am unused to banshees crying Boo at me.
Your wife can't be a banshee,
Or can she?
Of course, some wives become less fond
When you're bottled in bond.
My Uncle George, in lavender-scented Aunt Edna's
   day,
If he had a glass of beer on Saturday night, he didn't
   dare come home till the following Wednesday.
I see now that he had hit upon the ideal idea,
The passage of time, and plenty of it, is the only
   marital panacea.
Ah, if the passage of time were backward, and last
   night I'd been a child again, this morning I'd be
   fragrant with orange juice,

Instead of reeking of pinch-bottle foreign juice;
But if I should turn out to be a child again, what
    would life hold for me?
The woman I love would be too old for me.
There's only one solution to my problem, a hair of
    the dog, or maybe a couple of hairs;
Then if she doesn't get mad at me life will be peace-
    ful, and if she does it will show she really cares.

TO MY VALENTINE

More than a catbird hates a cat,
Or a criminal hates a clue,
Or an odalisque hates the Sultan's mates,
That's how much I love you.

I love you more than a duck can swim,
And more than a grapefruit squirts,
I love you more than commercials are a bore,
And more than a toothache hurts.

As a shipwrecked sailor hates the sea,
Or a juggler hates a shove,
As a hostess detests unexpected guests,
That's how much you I love.

I love you more than a wasp can sting,
And more than the subway jerks,
I love you truer than a toper loves a brewer,
And more than a hangnail irks.

I love you more than a bronco bucks,
Or a Yale man cheers the Blue.
Ask not what is this thing called love;
It's what I'm in with you.

THOUGHTS THOUGHT
ON AN AVENUE

There would be far less masculine gaming and booz-
    ing
But for the feminine approach to feminine fashions,
    which is distinctly confusing.
Please correct me if, although I don't think I do, I
    err;
But it is a fact that a lady wants to be dressed ex-
    actly like everybody else but she gets pretty up-
    set if she sees anybody else dressed exactly like
    her.
Nothing so infuriates her as a similar hat or dress,
Especially if bought for less,
Which brings up another point which I will attempt
    to discuss in my guttural masculine jargon:
Her ideal raiment is costlier than her or her dearest
    friend's purse can buy, and at the same time her
    own exclusive and amazing bargain.
Psychologists claim that men are the dreamers and
    women are the realists,
But to my mind women are the starriest-eyed of
    idealists,
Though I am willing to withdraw this charge and
    gladly eat it uncomplaineously

If anyone can explain to me how a person can wear a costume that is different from other people's and the same as other people's, and more expensive than other people's and cheaper than other people's, simultaneously.

THE TROUBLE WITH
WOMEN IS MEN

A husband is a man who two minutes after his head
    touches the pillow is snoring like an overloaded
    omnibus,
Particularly on those occasions when between the
    humidity and the mosquitoes your own bed is no
    longer a bed but an insomnibus,
And if you turn on the light for a little reading he
    is sensitive to the faintest gleam,
But if by any chance you are asleep and he wakeful,
    he is not slow to rouse you with the complaint
    that he can't close his eyes, what about slipping
    downstairs and freezing him a cooling dish of
    pistachio ice cream.
His touch with a bottle opener is sure,
But he cannot help you get a tight dress over your
    head without catching three hooks and a button
    in your coiffure.
Nor can he so much as wash his ears without leaving
    an inch of water on the bathroom linoleum,
But if you mention it you evoke not a promise to
    splash no more but a mood of deep melanchol-
    ium.

Indeed, each time he transgresses your chance of correcting his faults grows lesser,

Because he produces either a maddeningly logical explanation or a look of martyrdom which leaves you instead of him feeling the remorse of the transgressor.

Such are husbandly foibles, but there are moments when a foible ceases to be a foible.

Next time you ask for a glass of water and when he brings it you have a needle almost threaded and instead of setting it down he stands there holding it out to you, just kick him fairly hard in the stomach, you will find it thoroughly enjoible.

A WORD TO HUSBANDS

To keep your marriage brimming,
With love in the loving cup,
Whenever you're wrong, admit it;
Whenever you're right, shut up.

THE UNSELFISH HUSBAND

Once upon a time there was a man named Orlando
Tregennis and he was in love with his wife,
And he thought he would express his love by serenad-
ing her, but his serenade wasn't very successful
because his playing interfered with his singing
because all he could play was the fife,
So then he said, I will climb the highest mountain in
the world and name it after my wife and then she
will give me a look of love, so he climbed the
highest mountain in the world and his wife was
indeed whom he named it after,
But she didn't give him a look of love, she gave him
a look of laughter,
And not only a look of laughter but a look of menace,
Because he named it after his wife by naming it Mt.
Mrs. Orlando Tregennis,
So then he said that he certainly was sorry that during the first war he had absentmindedly forgot-
ten to join the army,
Because he said if he had been entitled to a bonus he
would have given her every penny even though
she was already so entrancing that no amount
of mere money could make her a jot or tittle
more allury or charmy,

And she greeted this remark with ribald merriment,

And she said that possibly money wouldn't get her
any further than she was, but she'd like a chance
to try the experiment,

So then Mr. Tregennis said, Well, I haven't any gold,

But I will give you my most precious possession, I
will give you my cold,

And he gave her his cold and first of all she tried to
spurn it,

And then she tried to return it,

But he said, No, darling, now it's your very own cold,

It is yours to have and to hold,

Because if you reckon I don't give gifts for keeps you
made a mistake when you reckoned,

Because there hasn't been an Indian-giver in the Tregennis family since my great-great-grandfather,
old Hiawatha Tregennis II.

But she wouldn't take no for an answer, but he
wouldn't say yes, and Mr. Tregennis's precious
cold went shuttling back and forth between them
for the rest of their lives,

And I hope everybody will turn out to be such self-
sacrificing husbands and wives.

THE ANNIVERSARY

A marriage aged one
Is hardly begun;
A fling in the sun,
But it's hardly begun;
A green horse,
A stiff course,
And leagues to be run.

A marriage aged five
Is coming alive.
Watch it wither and thrive;
Though it's coming alive,
You must guess,
No or yes,
If it's going to survive.

A marriage aged ten
Is a hopeful Amen;
It's pray for it then,
And mutter Amen,
As the names
Of old flames
Sound again and again.

At twenty a marriage
Discovers its courage.
This year do not disparage,
It is comely in courage;
Past the teens
And blue jeans,
It's a promising marriage.

Yet before twenty-one
It has hardly begun.
How tall in the sun,
Yet hardly begun!
But once come of age,
Pragmatically sage,
Oh, blithe to engage
Is sweet marri-age.

Tilt a twenty-first cup
To a marriage grown up,
Now sure and mature,
And securely grown up.
Raise twenty-one cheers
To the silly young years,
While I sit out the dance
With my dearest of dears.

IT'S ABOUT TIME

How simple was the relationship between the sexes in
    the days of Francesca di Rimini;
Men were menacing, women were womeny.
When confronted with women, men weren't expected
    to understand them;
Their alternatives were, if accepted, to embrace, if
    rejected, to unhand them.
I attribute much of our modern tension
To a misguided striving for intersexual comprehen-
    sion.
It's about time to realize, brethren, as best we can,
That a woman is not just a female man.
How bootless, then, to chafe
When they are late because they have no watch with
    them, all eleven of their watches are on the dress-
    ing table or in the safe;
How fruitless to pout
Because they believe that every time the dog
    scratches it really wants to go out;
Give your tongue to the cat
When you ask what they want for their birthday and
    they say, Oh anything, and you get anything,
    and then discover it should have been anything
    but that.
Pocket the gold, fellows, ask not why it glisters;

As Margaret Fuller accepted the universe, so let us
   accept her sisters.
Women would I think be easier nationalized
Than rationalized,
And the battle of the sexes can be a most enjoyable
   scrimmage
If you'll only stop trying to create woman in your
   own image.

HOW CAN ECHO ANSWER
WHAT ECHO CANNOT HEAR?

Why shouldn't I laud my love?
My love is highly laudable;
Indeed, she would be perfection
Were she only always audible.

Why shouldn't I laud her voice,
The welcomest sound I know,
Her voice, which is ever soft?
It is likewise gentle and low —

An excellent thing in woman
And the Wilson's thrush, or veery —
But there are maddening moments
When I wish I had wed a Valkyrie.

Whenever her talk is restricted
To topics inconsequential
She utters it face to face,
With clarity reverential.

Then why, when there's something important to say,
Does she always say it going away?
She'll remark, as she mounts the stairs to bed,
"Oh, some FBI man called and said . . ."

Then her words, like birds too swift for banding,
Vanish with her upon the landing.
"Don't you think we ought . . ." Then she's gone,
      whereat
The conclusion fades out like the Cheshire Cat.
Yes, her words when weighty with joy or dread
Seem to emerge from the back of her head;
The dénouement supreme, the point of the joke,
Is forever drifting away like smoke.
Knowing her custom, knowing the wont of her,
I spend my life circling to get in front of her.

I'll bet that the poet Herrick,
With Corinna gone a-Maying,
Had to run like a rabbit
To catch what she was saying.

FRAILTY, THY NAME
IS A MISNOMER

Once there was a couple named Mr. and Mrs. Pepper-
loaf and they were simply devoted,
Because each other was upon what they doted,
And in Mrs. Pepperloaf's eyes Mr. Pepperloaf could
never err,
And he admitted only one flaw in her,
But it was a flaw which took many virtues to assuage,
Consisting in always asking him the date while she
was reading the paper with the date clearly
printed on every page,
And whenever he called her attention to this least ad-
mirable of her traits
She would retort that he didn't trust the paper's
weather forecasts so then why should she trust
its dates.
For eleven years his patience held
But finally he rebelled.
It was on the evening of Friday the seventh that she
looked up from her paper and asked him the
date,
And he replied firmly that she would find it at the top
of the page, so she looked at the top of the page
and that was that, and presently they sat down
to supper and ate,

And they were miserable because they had never dis-
agreed and this contretemps was a beginner for
them,

And at nine his employer's wife called up to ask where
were they, she and eleven guests were waiting
dinner for them,

And Mr. Pepperloaf asked Mrs. Pepperloaf how she
could have so misreckoned,

And she said she knew that they had been invited out
on the seventh, but according to the newspaper
he had instructed her to consult tonight was
only the second,

And he picked up the paper and it was last week's,
not today's,

And she said certainly, she had just been keeping it
to read over some recipes for different delicious
soufflés,

And now she found the first flaw in him, because she
had obeyed his order to look for the date in the
paper, hadn't she, so his irritation was uncalled
for and unseasonable.

Women would rather be right than reasonable.

THE MIDDLE

When I remember bygone days
I think how evening follows morn;
So many I loved were not yet dead,
So many I love were not yet born.

HOW TO BE MARRIED
WITHOUT A SPOUSE
OR
MR. KIPLING, WHAT HAVE
YOU DONE WITH
MR. HAUKSBEE?

Do any of you old fogies remember Mrs. Hauksbee?
    Without Mrs. Hauksbee, Simla and Poona
Would have been just like Altoona.
At Mrs. Hauksbee's *burra khanas*
Nabobs pinned tails on donkeys and viceroys bobbed
    for bananas.
Mrs. Hauksbee disentangled subalterns and aides-de-
    camp
From shopworn maids-de-camp.
Under the deodars, whatever they may be, Mrs.
  Hauksbee was in her glory,
But this is another story.
Mrs. Hauksbee was attended by a faithful old *amah*,
Which is the equivalent of in Alabama a faithful old
    mamah,
And this now *amah* was a conservative reactionary
    Hindu,
And she got tired of Mrs. Hauksbee all the time shift-
    ing her hemline and her hair-do and her skin-do,

And finally she asked Mrs. Hauksbee why she had
   dyed her hair again and she got one of the usual
   answers.
Mrs. Hauksbee said she was changing her style to re-
   form young Slingsby of the Umpteenth Lancers,
And the *amah* (she had surreptitiously attended the
   Sorbonne)
Murmured, *"Plus ça change, plus c'est la memsahib,"*
   and wandered on.

THE STRANGE CASE OF
MR. DONNYBROOK'S
BOREDOM

Once upon a time there was a man named Mr. Donnybrook.

ↄↄ

He was married to a woman named Mrs. Donnybrook.

ↄↄ

Mr. and Mrs. Donnybrook dearly loved to be bored.

ↄↄ

Sometimes they were bored at the ballet, other times
at the cinema.

ↄↄ

They were bored riding elephants in India and ele-
vators in the Empire State Building.

ↄↄ

They were bored in speakeasies during Prohibition
and in cocktail lounges after Repeal.

ↄↄ

They were bored by Grand Dukes and garbagemen,
debutantes and demimondaines, opera singers
and Onassises.

ↄↄ

They scoured the Five Continents and the Seven Seas in their mad pursuit of boredom.

☙

This went on for years and years.

☙

One day Mr. Donnybrook turned to Mrs. Donnybrook,

☙

My dear, he said, we have reached the end of our rope.

☙

We have exhausted every yawn.

☙

The world holds nothing more to jade our titillated palates.

☙

Well, said Mrs. Donnybrook, we might try insomnia.

☙

So they tried insomnia.

☙

About two o'clock the next morning Mr. Donnybrook said, My, insomnia is certainly quite boring, isn't it?

☙

Mrs. Donnybrook said it certainly was, wasn't it?

☙

Mr. Donnybrook said it certainly was.

☙

Pretty soon he began to count sheep.

Mrs. Donnybrook began to count sheep, too.

After a while Mr. Donnybrook said, Hey, you're counting my sheep!

Stop counting my sheep, said Mr. Donnybrook.

Why, the very idea, said Mrs. Donnybrook.

I guess I know my own sheep, don't I?

How? said Mr. Donnybrook.

They're cattle, said Mrs. Donnybrook.

They're cattle, and longhorns at that.

Furthermore, said Mrs. Donnybrook, us cattle ranchers is shore tired o' you sheepmen plumb ruinin' our water.

I give yuh fair warnin', said Mrs. Donnybrook, yuh better git them woolly Gila monsters o' yourn back across the Rio Grande afore mornin' or I'm a-goin' to string yuh up on the nearest cottonwood.

❧

Carramba! sneered Mr. Donnybrook. Thees ees free range, no?

❧

No, said Mrs. Donnybrook, not for sheepmen.

❧

She strung him up on the nearest cottonwood.

❧

Mr. Donnybrook had never been so bored in his life.

MY DREAM

Here is a dream.
It is my dream,
My own dream,
I dreamt it.
I dreamt that my hair was kempt,
Then I dreamt that my true love unkempt it.

DON'T WAIT, HIT ME NOW!

If there are any wives present who wish to irritate
    their husbands or husbands who wish to irritate
    their wives,
Why, I know an irritation more irritating than hives,
So if you think such an irritation expedient,
Here is the formula, in which the presence of a third
    person is the only essential extra ingredient;
Indeed it is beautifully simple,
But it is guaranteed to make a molehill out of a
    dimple,
And what it consists of is that when you are annoyed
    with your husband or wife and want to do the
    opposite of woo them,
Why, you just talk at them instead of to them.
Suppose you think your Gregory danced too often
    with Mrs. Limbworthy at the club, you don't
    say to him directly, "Gregory, I'll smack you
    down if you don't lay off that platinum-plated
    hussy,"
No, you wait till a friend drops in and then with a
    glance at Gregory say to her, "Isn't it funny
    what fools middle-aged men can make of them-
    selves over anything blonde and slithery, do you

99

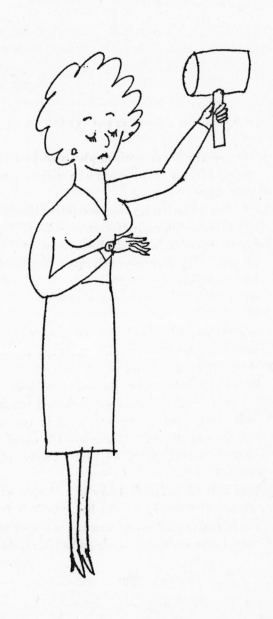

understand how anybody sober and in their
right mind could look twice at that Limbworthy
job, but then of course darling, Gregory wasn't
altogether in his right mind last night, was he?"
This is indeed more excruciating to Gregory than
Shakespearian excursions and alarums,
Because there is no defense against caroms.
Or let us suppose you are irked by your Esmeralda's
sudden passion for antiques,
Well, you don't mention it for weeks,
No, you wait till a friend drops in and then with a
glance at Esmeralda you say, "How anybody
can be sucked in by this antique racket is beyond
me, but there are some otherwise sensible women
who'll mortgage their beauty treatments for a
genuine secondhand Killarney banshee,
But of course Esmeralda can't ever resist an opportunity to pick up some fossil to amaze her
friends with, can she?"
And Esmeralda must sit quiet and take it with ap-
parent docility,
Because the hit direct doesn't compare with the rico-
chet in deadly unanswerability.
By this easy method can every Gregory score off
every Esmeralda and every Esmeralda annihilate
every Gregory,
And its only drawback besides eventual divorce is
that it reduces all their friends to emotional
beggary.

THE WINNER

Ecstatic poets through the ages
Have writ their love on golden pages,
Treading on one another's toes
Till Bartlett brims and overflows,
And all their memorable phrases
Are common as goldenrod or daisies.
Why should I vie with such, my sweet,
When I descry in you, complete,
That ultimate sonnet, sunset-bright,
That Shakespeare always meant to write?

COME ON IN,
THE SENILITY IS FINE

People live forever in Jacksonville and St. Petersburg
 and Tampa,
But you don't have to live forever to become a
 grampa.
The entrance requirements for grampahood are com-
 paratively mild,
You only have to live until your child has a child.
From that point on you start looking both ways over
 your shoulder,
Because sometimes you feel thirty years younger and
 sometimes thirty years older.
Now you begin to realize who it was that reached the
 height of imbecility,
It was whoever said that grandparents have all the
 fun and none of the responsibility.
This is the most enticing spiderweb of a tarradiddle
 ever spun,
Because everybody would love to have a baby around
 who was no responsibility and lots of fun,
But I can think of no one but a mooncalf or a gaby
Who would trust their own child to raise a baby.
So you have to personally superintend your grand-
 child from diapers to pants and from bottle to
 spoon,

Because you know that your own child hasn't sense
enough to come in out of a typhoon.
You don't have to live forever to become a grampa,
but if you do want to live forever,
Don't try to be clever;
If you wish to reach the end of the trail with an
uncut throat,
Don't go around saying Quote I don't mind being a
grampa but I hate being married to a gramma
Unquote.

CROSSING THE BORDER

Senescence begins
And middle age ends
The day your descendants
Outnumber your friends.

ONCE MORE
TO MY VALENTINE

Just five and thirty years ago
I walked alone on earth,
That callous, carefree creature,
A bachelor from birth.
No thrill of premonition,
No tingling of the spine
Foreshadowed the appearance
Of my only valentine.

I had no thought of courtship
At that far-distant date;
One girl was like another,
So why, then, concentrate?
One pearl was like another
To this self-centered swine
Who was surfeited with sameness
And knew no valentine.

Just five and thirty years ago
I danced with mind astray,
And suddenly the sameness
Was forever swept away.
I hardly heard the music
I couldn't taste the wine,
For, lovely as a legend,
I saw my valentine.

Oh, lovely as a legend,
Or a silver birch in spring,
And haunting as the twilight song
That hidden thrushes sing!
How I elbowed through my fellows
As they stood in penguin line!
How I dodged among the dancers
As I sought my valentine!

The orchestra played waltzes,
Blank faces swirled about;
I have no foot for waltzes,
So we sat the waltzes out.
Came the tunes of Kern and Gershwin,
But I liked the terrace fine;
Till the band played "Good Night, Ladies,"
I wooed my valentine.

Just five and thirty years ago
I walked the earth alone,
The shortest five and thirty years
That earth has ever known.
Young love is well remembered,
But why long for old lang syne
When tonight she is beside me,
My beloved valentine,
My fairest valentine,
My dearest valentine,
Through five and thirty precious years
My own true valentine.